The CEO Stylist

Hairdressers About Business

LaKeisha Michelle

Table of Contents

Foreword

The beauty industry is a Multi-Billion Dollar one, and it's only growing. LaKeisha Michelle has captured the game-changing techniques that is the path to

-3X your revenue growth

-create the time and freedom you want

-turn what could feel like your hustle into your business enterprise.

Many people talk about building a 6-figure business, but LaKeisha Michelle has a proven track record. Many people will become stylist, but only a few will change the game and become The CEO Stylist. Hook your caboose to this firehouse's train, hold on tight, and get ready for drastic transformation!

-Lisa Nichols

CEO of Motivating the Masses

Introduction

So you graduated from beauty school. You had ideas. You had technical skills. But aside from that, what else did you have? What did you find yourself prepared for when you stepped out of school and stepped in that salon? Was there a big vision in the back of your mind? Did you have dreams of maybe going to Hollywood or being that hairstylist for Beyoncé, or the first lady? Or was it more practical?

For a lot of us, our vision was just simply getting by and having a life. We looked at an amount that—maybe now we even realize how small it was—but then it just seemed like that would be the end, like that would be the best if we could just get to that. So, we stepped out into that beauty school and stepped into our lives as a stylist. But if you're anything like me, you've stepped into a world that you're totally unprepared for. You didn't know anything other than technical skills. So, what I want to share with you today is how much of a CEO you need to be in order to be the stylist that you can be.

The truth of the matter is, as stylists, we do have a powerful impact on the world around us. And if we're committed to it, we can create that safe place where a person can go for an hour or two, sit in our chair, and have more than just a good conversation or a good hairstyle. We can create a place where they can just take off their cape, not have to be a 'super mom' all the time, and just be spoiled themselves. Think about it for a minute. What would be the best 1 to 2-hour break out of your life that you could take, and how could you create that environment for somebody else?

DESIGNING MY LIFE

Today, I show up in the world teaching and inspiring through content and song in two ways. I teach hair stylist online how to build six figure businesses. I also get paid to enhance live event experiences by fusing meaningful messages with customized or popular songs that inspire the heart, open the mind, and stir your soul. I had to learn the hard way how to run my businesses. I realized that there are so many places you can go to learn the technical skills for being a hair stylist, but most places aren't digging deep and teaching us the "business" of hair.

So, I took to my YouTube channel to talk about what being a CEO Stylist really looks like! I don't teach a theory. These are concepts that I have lived, applied, and gotten results. I want to help others learn that they really can choose the way they want their life to be. You don't have to be someone special with some award winning hair skill. All of us can design the life we want. I work when I want, earn what I want, and truly live the life I want. I now know how to manage the money, and see growth in the different areas of my business. In the past, I made a lot, spent a lot, and never knew where money would go at the end of the month. I was burned out. I had no clue how to budget, pay myself, taxes, assistants, distributors, etc. Certain customers were nightmares. I couldn't manage anything I'd created on any level. So unconsciously, I sabotaged everything I worked so hard for.

A PIVOTAL MOMENT

I'll never forget that day I was sitting behind my desk, looking at my bank account. I screamed in frustration to myself, "I'm finally making all kinds of money, and yet, I don't have any! WHERE IS MY MONEY?"

Have you ever been there? I wanted to do so much in the world, but I just couldn't. I couldn't help my family the way I wanted. I was so stressed financially, and I wasn't in control. I spent just as much as I made. I had all these things that "looked cool" but I was so broke. I didn't understand. Even though I was working on my feet all the time, and money was coming in, it was going out even quicker. I wondered why things weren't growing.

There I was at my desk, on my 26th birthday, looking at my money, and just feeling very tired. I said to myself, "I just can't take this anymore. I don't even want to celebrate my birthday. I don't want this business anymore." For me, that was a pivotal moment. I was disgusted. In that moment, I realized that I had to search for how to deal with finances. Even deeper, I had to search for \how to become the CEO and run my business. I needed to study me.

What was I doing that was working? What wasn't working? I found myself back learning what I'd originally attended college for - business management! I read books, attended conferences, hired coaches (with money I didn't have), and got advice from everyone doing better than me to figure out solutions to better run my business.

I kept working, but I also realized I needed something even more drastic that I couldn't shake. My mentor Lisa Nichols gave me some advice and told me that I needed to change my environment by moving out of Dallas and getting a fresh start. She said that I needed to begin taking care of myself. At first, I wasn't sure that I wanted to do that. I had that pit in my stomach and was scared senseless, but I decided to go ahead and save a little money and take that leap of faith. I moved to California! As I look back now, moving to California really helped me to fix my life. When I first moved to California, I actually quit doing hair for a while because I couldn't manage it. I just concentrated on my music and being an independent artist. After six months, I realized that as fun as it was, I needed more money to fund this musical journey. So I went back to the hair styling business, but this time I wanted to test and see if I could build a six-figure business again in a new city where no one knew me, using my CEO Stylist formula.

Within a year, my numbers were back to the six-figure mark, and I was working very little hours in the salon. I became committed to doing business with grace and ease. I was determined to learn from the things that I'd done wrong and become the true CEO of my business and my life.

I had a formula that was fail proof.

It worked! It worked better and faster than I could have ever imagined. Even before I left Dallas, I'd been testing certain aspects of my system on other hairdressers. I taught courses teaching how to build websites, how to use YouTube to get sales, and more. My results for myself and everyone else was working! I just decided to piece it all together. My favorite thing is waking up to messages from hair stylist that say they have gotten results, or that I've helped end the confusion and anxiety they had because they didn't understand where things went wrong in their business.

WORK ON THE BUSINESS, NOT JUST IN THE BUSINESS

I look back at the amazing opportunity I had shortly after graduating cosmetology school in 2010. I won a contest where L'Oreal picked 6 out of over 250 applicants from across the country to travel all over the United States for six months - all expenses paid! Our job was to blog about everything we learned while they literally showed us the "ins and outs" of the entire industry. We were mentored by some of the most famous hairdressers all over the world. This was a major moment in my life. I even wrote and sold my first song for a large sum to them during this time.

I went to a different state every week, and multiple cities in each state. Something I saw that was lacking so much in the industry was vision. At all the schools we visited, which were minimum three or four each week, the main focus was passing state board and the technical side of doing hair. In the salons we visited, hairdressers were tired, and just at work. A lot were passionate, but had no clue what they could really create in their lives.

I remember finding a book while I was in beauty school that changed my life. It was called, "Eat That Frog" by Brian Tracy. One of the things he talked about was stating your goals and then speaking them as if they'd already happened. Using his strategies was the way I actually made money right out of beauty school. I just told myself "Just do what he says." This book opened me up to another world!

I was on fire and shared my learnings with everyone each week. People were in awe. I saw that the conversation of how to really run a business isn't something that's loud enough. It's not like you get a 12-week course on business while you're in beauty school.

We don't have enough conversations about how to generate, manage, and grow our revenue. Sadly, all over the country I saw this. I took to my YouTube and started sharing my discoveries. My learnings opened my view to how things are run, and the possibilities of 'what could be' if we simply took the time to realize that we need to work on the business, and not just in the business.

THE CEO FACTOR

Ever since I can remember, I've been interested in the different aspects of business. When I got into the hair business, I did so much market research by simply asking ladies everywhere – an event, church, Walmart, etc. - what they were looking for. I took notes and adjusted my work. It was so natural for me.

I loved reading books and studying different topics like marketing; sales; customer service; technology; and more. From the age 20 to 29, I've researched all the things that weren't in that Milady's Cosmetology book! I hate to say it, but a lot of the instructors I encountered loved to teach, and they were great, but they hadn't built six or seven figure businesses. Trust me, I have met hundreds of hairdressers all over the United States, and they just didn't have that experience to share. They are valuable and get us far, but most don't have what I call "The CEO Factor."

Part of being a successful CEO is having a vision. You need to have a vision—both for your company and your life. Ask yourself different types of questions like, "What direction is this company going to take? How are you going to approach customer service? Are you willing to do what it takes, to not just function in your business but really grow it? What is the environment around your station in your salon look like? Is it comfortable? Is it a place that you want to go where you would feel relaxed? Or is it very clean and technical, like a place where you can get the job done, but doesn't really make a person feel at home and comfortable?"

In my own experience, I became laser-focused on my customers. I started thinking about what I can do to make sure that their experience is a unique one and to consistently show them a way to enjoy their time. On the back end, I had to start looking at my numbers consistently every day. What did I make? What did I spend? What were my highest selling items? I also realized the answer wasn't "If I could just get more customers" like most stylists think. I was finally seeing how my actions were affecting my business. I found that I love going deeper and serving higher with a select few. As a result, I worked less, made more, and loved my days in the salon.

VISION FOR MY CLIENTS

You see, a CEO has several very important traits, but all of them boil down to having a bigger vision for the company. A good, successful and effective CEO knows his/her targets. CEOs have a clear direction of where they want to go. They are self-disciplined enough to focus on going for the vision that they have. Everything that a CEO does is in alignment with this particular 'bigger vision'. We must operate with integrity to show the customer that they are important. Do we let our clients know that we care about them? Do we show them that we're on time, or that we have a drink ready for them? Do we treat them in the way that we want to be treated? Do we make them feel that we're there to get them the things they need? For me, if I see a client looking around with a cup in their hand, I would run and grab them a coaster or tray so they have a place to set their drink. I serve them. I can't stress this enough. We need to make sure they're comfortable.

You see, as a CEO, you have to have a vision not only for the business but also for your clients. You have to have a vision for what their experience can be like. If not, I can tell you from experience that you will go down the same road that I did. At the end of that road you're so overwhelmed that the only solution you see is that you've got to stop this. If you don't manage your business, your business will manage you. So I encourage you to measure everything. Begin to adjust every two weeks on all of the details. Evaluate everything. Ask yourself, "Who did I talk to this last week? Who called me back? What things on my marketing, sales, or interaction with my customers are working and what things aren't? What can I change so that I could be more impactful and more effective, both with my clients but also in dealing with my business?" A lot of these things boil down to knowing your numbers. It's more than just counting how many clients you had that week. It has to do with being able to say "I spent this much money on my marketing budget this week which brought in this number of clients, and those clients spent this much." Whereas, maybe the next week you spend the money that you did in marketing last week, on something else and it doesn't work as well. And then you will know if you need to either change what you're doing in that marketing or not use that again.

Another question you should ask yourself is, "What am I paying my employees?" In my experience, I remember hiring an assistant and paying them way too much because I didn't know any better. The money was flowing through the business so I didn't realize how much of it I was putting out in ways that weren't serving the business. I had just looked at the people that were working around me and saw what they were doing after I graduated, and so I just did what they did. There was this lady who had a long line of people backed all the way down the block wanting to come to her. So, what was she doing? Some of those things were very effective, especially technically, but what I found was that when I really started to do that myself, I also needed to have the business skills to control my money. Although I was bringing in a lot of money, it was being sent right back out the door as quickly as it was coming into the cash register. If I knew then what I know now, I know I would have had even higher numbers.

GET CLEARER

So what can you do? You've heard me say it before, but I'm going to say it again. The number one thing you need is to get a vision. Your salon should be that thing that you're using to get you to the life you want. If you don't know what life you want, how will you know if you're heading there?

So stop for a second and really think about the life you want. While I can't paint that for you, I can tell you that whatever you have dreamed of can and will happen for you. You don't need to know the how and when. What I do know for a fact is that you just need to write the vision and make it plain.

Don't feel silly when you look into your future. Don't feel like you don't have what it takes. Don't feel like you have to wait until you are like "so and so" to be qualified to dream big. Your waking up is enough. This is not hype, this is REAL talk. I live this. Before I ever knew how, I told myself I would live by the beach and drive a drop top Jeep. Before I ever knew how, I said I would sell music to people all over the world. Before I moved to California, I said I would write a book one day. Before I knew how, I said I would be on yachts in other countries living the life.

It all happened, and I'm here to tell you to dream big! Your personal vision must be clear because your business is a means to get you to the life you want. Get quiet. Turn off the news and radio. Stop watching reality shows wishing, and figure out what you want, and be unapologetic.

Where will you live? How much money do you take home from your business monthly?

What does your dream home look like? Where do you shop? What vacations do you take? Where do your children go to school? How have you been able to support your family? What kind of car do you drive? What and who are you able to be because of how you show up in your business world?!

This is huge. Get that vision clear and big enough that it scares you, then go back and look at your business. Can it give you this life? Have you mapped out what your business really looks and feels like for the customer? What will keep them coming back? What feeling should they leave your salon with every time?

Look at your actions daily in the business. Does your marketing videos and images match your business vision? For example, I like taking the everyday woman and giving her hope, sass, and timeless class. My marketing images are things like women 40 and up, looking out into the beach. I want my ideal client to be inspired. That matches my vision for my life, my clients, and my salon business.

Let me be clear, you have to take this thing all the way down to the shampoo brands and even the chairs. With that vision for my clients, I can't do things like use cheap salon products. All the small details create that big picture we see. Revisit what you are selling, and see if the price points align with the kind of customer you envision serving. Does the price point get you to the lifestyle you dream? Does the price point allow you to serve your clients in the way that they need? Are you even doing the services that you want to be doing? Or are you selling services that somebody told you to sell?

Once you get clear on your vision, you will notice a fire and excitement inside of you. You will want to share it with everyone around you. Always remember that clarity of vision, and living with purpose focused towards that vision, are key. For me, transitioning from just doing what I thought I should do- to really taking the time to know my vision for my company and heading that way- made all the difference.

DISCIPLINE AND MARKETING

Another trait that a CEO needs to have is discipline. Often, we get so tied down to the 'how' part that we forget what we need to do. We need to be disciplined and stay focused on what our target is, so that we are doing the things that serve our business. Often we do the things that are distracting us from that target. Discipline is all about setting goals and knowing how to adjust. Whether that be on your marketing, the way you handle customers, your pricing, or anything to do with your sales. The discipline is that thing that has you looking at your numbers every week, adjusting every one of the details so that you end up with the company that you wanted in that vision. Discipline is what takes us there.

For an instance, I believe you need at least three marketing strategies and a plan on how are you going to execute each one. Get deep. What time of the day are you marketing to people on Facebook? What days of the week do you need to be standing out with flyers at Target? When and what time do you need to go on YouTube live each week? What kinds of videos do you need to share in order to build your business? All of those things are what you need to do on purpose when we talk about marketing. Marketing isn't something that happens accidentally. And if you're going to rely just on word of mouth from people, you're going to end up in a situation that you can't control. Yes, some people are going to say amazing things about you, but others—even the ones that are trying to say good things—aren't going to be saying those things that you really want clients to say out there in the world. So we have to market on purpose and always measure what impact our marketing strategies have on our business. Never stop marketing. Be loud. Be seen. Stay booked.

The thing I want you to understand is that without discipline you won't stick to anything. And it's imperative to have structure on things like your finances and marketing. So many stylists I consult with, tell me when they started they were booming, but one day they looked up and customers were sparse. It was all because there was no ongoing marketing and sales strategy. Maybe you're doing some things here and there to market but there is no discipline in your marketing schedule. Go over those questions I listed above and get a schedule. Stick to it!

Discipline is what you have to have in order to effectively manage time; finances; customers; products; and more. Businesses make money when they sell services or products. In order to sell, you have to market it. Marketing is how you tell your ideal customer what you do (or your vision for them). You must understand and learn to apply this concept to every step you make daily in your business.

You see, once a CEO has a clear vision, he is constantly looking and adjusting the company so that they are headed towards their destination. To not act that way is to be like the person who just gets in the car and starts driving, hoping he ends up in Miami, but finds himself in Kansas. Driving without a GPS works sometimes. You'll end up somewhere, but not necessarily where you intended to go. You don't want that to happen in your business. You need to have vision and discipline, and then measure, just like a GPS, each step as you travel to where you're going.

You see, the right vision will get you in alignment with everything else in your life and in your business. As I began looking at other businesses outside of being a stylist, what I found was massive. But these factors I've just shared with you I saw constant in any industry. When I found that I could write my vision; set goals; be disciplined; market myself; measure everything; and adjust and grow, it almost seems too simple. I began to test it both for myself and with the other hairdressers that I teach. Amazingly, the same business practices work in our beauty world.

CHANGING OUR WHOLE VIEW

I'm so grateful for the beauty industry. When I went to beauty school, I was broke and very depressed coming out of a horrible relationship. I didn't really take care of myself diligently. I was the furthest thing you could imagine from a CEO. I remember one of the teachers telling me, "What are you doing walking around looking like that?" At first, I was very offended and I didn't really want to change who I thought I was. But as time went by, I began to embrace my visions and realized I had to align myself with where I was going. I found myself on YouTube, looking up how to create videos, learning how I can present myself, taking whatever I had and making it look decent. I began to create an environment so that the vision that I had for my life and my business was reflected in everything that I did.

Being in the beauty industry has literally changed everything in my life. It changed my whole view—from a girl who was broke, and broken down by a guy, to somebody who has a large unfathomable vision, that wants to tell the world all about it. Remember guys, your vision should excite you into action. People stick with me because I'm constantly sharing everything I'm learning—with my clients, other hairdressers, family members, anyone who will listen. I will spend the rest of my days teaching and singing empowering content to people. As I do this work I see that 'light bulb' in their eyes as they begin to get their own visions and start to grow.

That's what I want for you, too. I want you, as a hairdresser, to have that same mindset as I now have. I want you to know that you are a person of vision, operating in excellence with discipline and that you can change the lives of the people around you. And really, by having that bigger vision, you can empower men and women, and change your little corner of the world. As hairdressers, we have a whole lot more power than we think. You're not just a salon owner, a hairdresser, or a stylist. Deep down, you're a businessman or businesswoman, a life changer, and a visionary. You are a CEO who is in control of the destiny of your life. I encourage you to embrace it. Live on fire in every aspect of what you do. Act like, think like, and be The CEO stylist.

If you want to continue this conversation I would love to meet you online. Ask questions. Say hello.

My favorite social media spots are YouTube, Facebook, or Instagram @LaKeishaMichelle.

For those game changing, action-taking hair stylists who are ready to implement these strategies and more, please visit www.theceostylist.com for a free video series that teaches critical steps you need to take to grow your business today!

www.ingramcontent.com/pod-product-compliance
Lightning Source LLC
Chambersburg PA
CBHW061801280526
45787CB00003BA/1438